CATHAL

CAN

SIGN

By Brenán Mooney

Introduction

The original idea for this book was to use visual communication to support the spoken word with babies and young children, hearing and hearing impaired, while integrating an early understanding of the three Irish languages, English, Gaelic and Irish Sign Language (ISL). Facial expressions and body language are an integral part of signing and lead to a greater depth of understanding and bonding between adult and child.

Vocalisation should be encouraged at all times and parents or carers should always speak when signing. Since speech is formed through the use of trained vocal chords, babies do no have the physical ability to speak but most babies can hear, so ISL is a wonderful way to communicate and encourage thought. Research has shown where early communication is established between adult and baby, the child's needs are met with no fuss and less frustration.

The mother and child relationship is primarily physical, but it includes visual and vocal interactions, and the benefits of this are early independence due to strong positive self confidence. Sign boosts social and emotional development, it encourages hand and eye coordination, as well as listening, play and expressive skills. Research also shows baby signers have more advanced verbal skills than non-signing babies.

Hello, my name is Cathal.

I can sign using sign language in **English** and **Gaelic**. Learning 3 languages is easy and fun. I can sign to all my **family,** and my **friends** know some sign too. My Mum taught me to sign when I was still a small **baby**. You can learn like me using this book.

Have fun!

Table of Contents

aibítir

Cathal's Alphabet

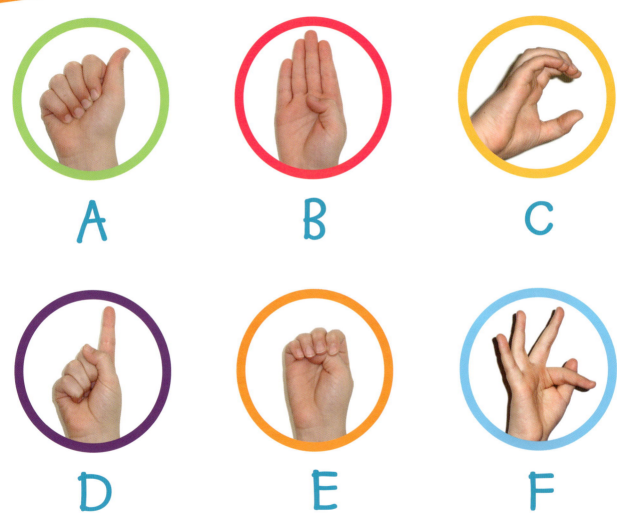

A

B

C

D

E

F

Cathal's Alphabet

G   H   I

J   K   L

Cathal's Alphabet

M N O

P Q R

Cathal's Alphabet

S

T

U

V

W

X

Cathal's Alphabet

Y

Z

clann

Cathal's Family

daddy

athair

mammy

máthair

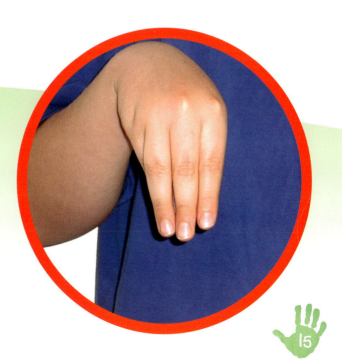

Cathal's Family

brother

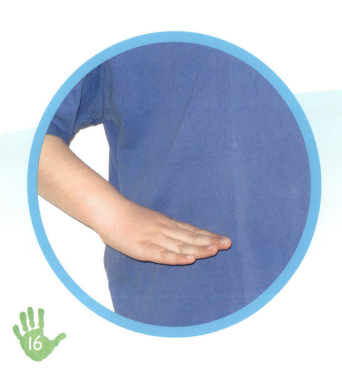

deartháir

Cathal's Family

sister

deirfiúr

17

grandfather

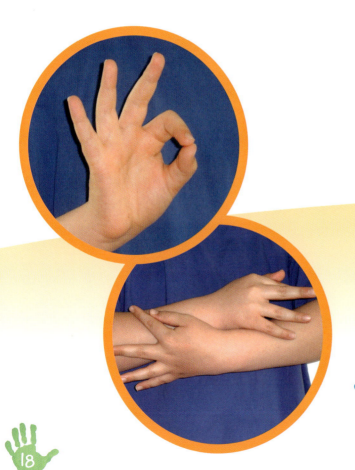

seanathair

18

Cathal's Family

grandmother

seanmháthair

19

baby

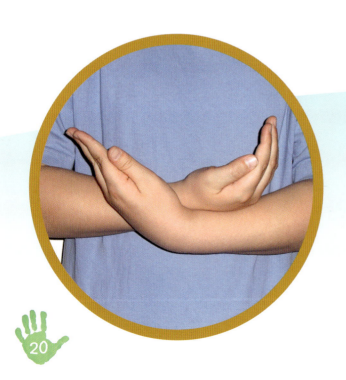

leanbh

20

dathanna

21

Cathal's Colours

black
dubh

white
bán

Cathal's Colours

red

dearg

blue

gorm

green
glas

yellow
buí

purple

corcra

27

orange

oráiste

Cathal's Colours

pink
bán-dearg

brown

donn

grey
liath

1 9 5 3 6 8 7 2 4 10

uimhreacha

32

Cathal's Numbers

1

one
aon

2

two
dó

33

Cathal's Numbers

3 three
trí

four
ceithre **4**

5

five

cúig

6

six

sé

Cathal's Numbers

7 seven
seacht

eight
ocht **8**

9 nine naoi

10 ten deich

aimsir

winter
an
geimhreadh

spring
an t-Earrach

39

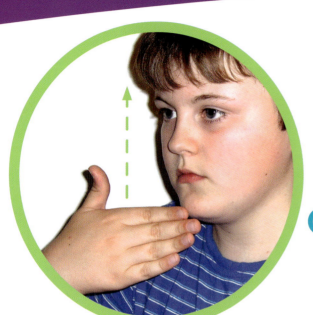

summer

an samhradh

40

autumn

an fómhar

Cathal's Weather

 rain
báisteach

sun
ghrian

 41

Cathal's Weather

wind
gaoth

cloud
scamall

42

CATHAL'S DAYS OF THE WEEK

leathanta
na seachtaine

Cathal's Days of the Week

monday

dé luain

tuesday

dé máirt

44

wednesday
dé céadaoin

thursday
déardaoin

45

Cathal's Days of the Week

friday

dé hAoine

saturday

dé sathairn

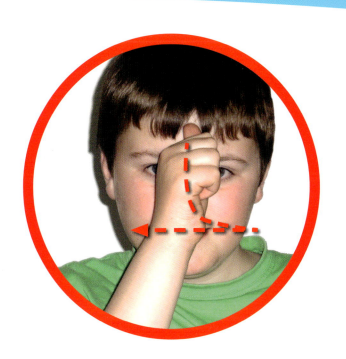

sunday

dé

domhnaigh

47

CATHAL'S FACE

aghaidh

Cathal's Face

eye
súil

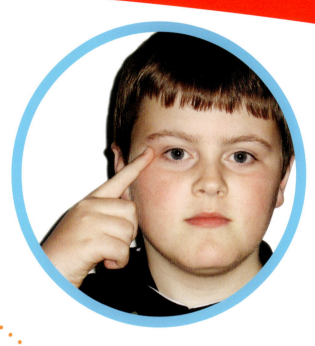

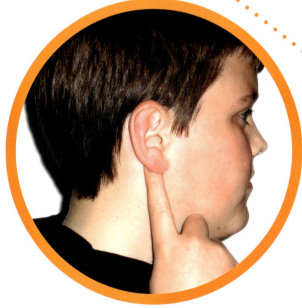

ear
cluas

49

Cathal's Face

nose

srón

mouth

béal

eyebrow

mala

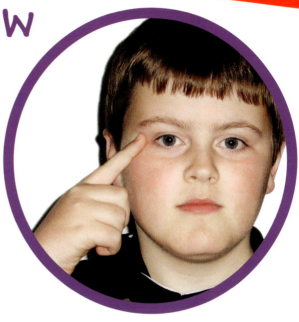

teeth

fiacla

51

focal

hello
dia dhuit

53

Cathal's Words

eat

ith

Cathal's Words

book
leabhar

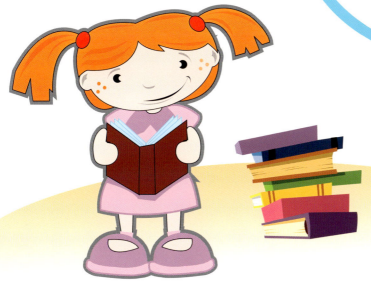

cake

cáca

Cathal's Words

sick
tinn

Cathal's Words

flower
bláth